Great Empires

The Chinese Empire

ELLIS ROXBURGH

WAYLAND

WAYLAND

www.waylandbooks.co.uk

Published in paperback in 2017 by Wayland

Copyright © 2015 Brown Bear Books Ltd

Wayland, an imprint of Hachette Children's Group
Part of Hodder & Stoughton
Carmelite House
50 Victoria Embankment
London EC4Y 0DZ
An Hachette UK Company
www.hachette.co.uk
www.hachettechildrens.co.uk

Dewey number: 909'.0971251-dc23
ISBN: 978 1 5263 0068 3
10 9 8 7 6 5 4 3 2 1

Brown Bear Books Ltd
First Floor
9–17 St Albans Place
London
N1 0NX

Editorial Director: Lindsey Lowe
Managing Editor: Tim Cooke
Children's Publisher: Anne O'Daly
Design Manager: Keith Davis
Designer: Melissa Roskell
Picture Manager: Sophie Mortimer
Production Director: Alastair Gourlay

Printed in China

Websites
The website addresses (URLs) included in this book were valid at the time of going to press. However, because of the nature of the internet, it is possible that some addresses may have changed, or sites may have changed or closed down since publication. While the author and publisher regret any inconvenience this may cause the readers, no responsibility for any such changes can be accepted by either the author or the publisher.

CONTENTS

Introduction

Over 3,500 years ago, the Shang became China's first great dynasty when they created a state on the Yellow River.

Virtually nothing was known about the Shang until the end of the 19th century, when a scholar discovered by chance old writing scraped into animal bones. These so-called **oracle bones** were the first physical evidence of the existence of a people who had, until then, been known only by their name appearing in ancient records. Nearly 100 years later, another spectacular breakthrough came with the discovery of a royal Shang tomb. The Tomb of Lady Hao provided more evidence of how the Shang lived. It also suggested that they had been of vital importance in the history of China.

The Shang heartlands on the plains of the Yellow River were bordered by vast mountain ranges that were difficult to cross.

The Shang were among the first people to cast metal objects by mixing copper and tin to create bronze, which was harder wearing than other metals.

Lack of Evidence

Despite a century of research, details of the Shang **dynasty** remain shrouded in mystery. There are no precise dates of the reigns of kings. Many Shang sites have been destroyed by the shifting course of the Yellow River (Huang He). Materials such as bamboo and silk have decomposed in over three millennia since the Shang flourished. Historians know the names of only a handful of royal individuals from the time and virtually nothing about the everyday lives of the Shang's subjects.

Influential Dynasty

Ongoing discoveries are adding to our understanding of the Shang all the time, but it is already clear that China's first dynasty played a remarkable role in shaping later Chinese culture. The Shang introduced bronze-working, developed an accurate calendar and created the first Chinese writing system. The Shang also introduced important ideas in Chinese religion. They foretold the future by practising divination, or reading signs including oracle bones. They also practised ancestor worship, which influenced the respect for family and seniority seen in Chinese faiths such as Confucianism and Taoism.

Oracle bones are one of the most important sources of information about the Shang. Priests interpreted cracks in shells and bones.

The Rule of the Shang

The Shang ruled a region of what is now north-eastern China for around 600 years, from about 1600 to 1046 BCE. The Shang were surrounded by neighbouring peoples, to whom they were very similar. The Shang did not really rule an empire in the usual sense of the word, in which a people impose their government on another people. Different Shang rulers did, however, expand their influence over their neighbours at different periods.

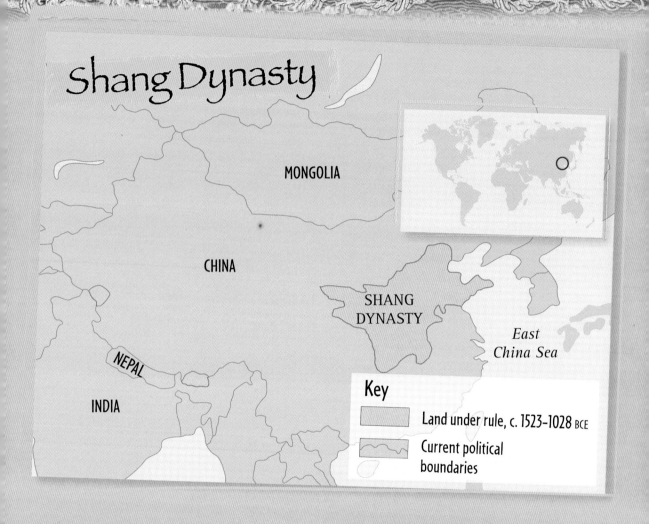

Shang Dynasty

MONGOLIA

CHINA

SHANG
DYNASTY

*East
China Sea*

NEPAL

INDIA

Key

Land under rule, c. 1523–1028 BCE

Current political
boundaries

They used military power to force states to become their
vassals and to send **tribute** to the Shang, often in the
form of grain.

Eventually, however, the Shang rulers grew corrupt. Their
subjects no longer supported them. In 1046 BCE, when a
people called the Zhou turned against their rulers, the last
Shang king killed himself. However, although the dynasty
may have ended long ago, its legacy still survives today.

The Roots of the Empire

The precise origins of the Shang dynasty are a mystery. However, archaeologists are slowly piecing together their history. The dynasty emerged along China's Yellow River around 1600 BCE.

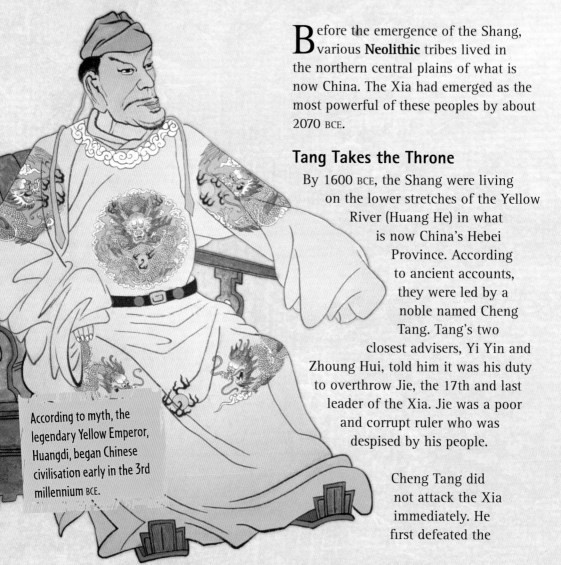

According to myth, the legendary Yellow Emperor, Huangdi, began Chinese civilisation early in the 3rd millennium BCE.

Before the emergence of the Shang, various **Neolithic** tribes lived in the northern central plains of what is now China. The Xia had emerged as the most powerful of these peoples by about 2070 BCE.

Tang Takes the Throne

By 1600 BCE, the Shang were living on the lower stretches of the Yellow River (Huang He) in what is now China's Hebei Province. According to ancient accounts, they were led by a noble named Cheng Tang. Tang's two closest advisers, Yi Yin and Zhoung Hui, told him it was his duty to overthrow Jie, the 17th and last leader of the Xia. Jie was a poor and corrupt ruler who was despised by his people.

Cheng Tang did not attack the Xia immediately. He first defeated the

The Yellow River winds across the plains. The river's frequent flooding created fertile land for farmers to grow crops.

neighbouring states of Ge, Wei, Gu and Kunwu, making the Shang the most powerful dynasty in the region. Cheng Tang was then in a position to challenge Jie.

Battle of Mingtiao

The armies of the Shang and the Xia met around 1600 BCE in the Battle of Mingtiao. The generals and soldiers of the Shang army loved Cheng Tang, but the Xia soldiers hated Jie and did not want to fight for him. The battle ended in an easy victory for the Shang.

Cheng Tang sent Jie into **exile** and the lords of all the neighbouring states swore loyalty to Cheng Tang, who became king

The Yellow River

The Chinese call the Yellow River (Huang He) the 'cradle of Chinese civilisation'. It supported many of China's earliest dynasties because the silt left by flooding made the land along the river extremely fertile. However, another nickname for the river is 'China's sorrow' because the silt has also caused catastrophic flooding over the centuries. The river's course has changed significantly since the time of the Shang.

The cult of the Yellow Emperor survives at Xuan Yuan Temple, although today historians credit many of his legendary inventions to the Shang.

KEY BELIEFS

Shang Di

Shang Di, the supreme god of the Shang, was thought to rule over the gods of the Sun, Moon, wind and rain. It was the job of the king to ask Shang Di's advice on everything from when to plant crops or go hunting to whether to go to war. Priests used oracle bones to interpret Shang Di's reply.

and founded the Shang dynasty. Since Cheng Tang was a noble, rather than a member of a royal family, some Chinese historians see this as the first example of a 'noble revolution'. Similar revolutions by nobles became a common way for new dynasties to start later in Chinese history.

Although the Shang **chronicles** say Cheng Tang had a duty to overthrow the corrupt Jie, there is no way of knowing what really happened. The Shang invented writing and were the first dynasty to leave a written record, so the account supports their view of the overthrow of the Xia.

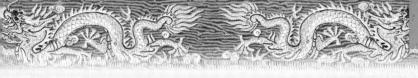
Coming of the Bronze Age

The lack of written evidence makes it difficult to know much about the Xia. Archaeological finds suggest that they were very similar to the Shang. At Erlitou, in what is now Henan Province, archaeologists have found a large imperial palace that was inhabited around 1700 BCE. It could have been built by either the early Shang dynasty or the Xia dynasty, leading some historians to suggest the two dynasties were in fact the same. Both these early Chinese cultures appeared to have a degree of sophistication. They learnt how to make objects out of **bronze**. They also both buried important people in tombs and built urban centres.

Archaeological Discovery

Almost nothing was known about the Shang until the chance discovery of some oracle bones in the late 19th century. Our knowledge of the early Shang and the Xia remains limited because it is rare to find sites or objects. Many Xia and Shang sites have been lost as the Yellow River changed course. When a site is discovered, very little has been found there except for some bronze tools.

A Shang royal cemetery has been excavated at Anyang in Henan Province, China. This was formerly the Shang capital Yin.

Building the Empire

The early Shang kings ruled China's first identifiable state. They organised their subjects to work on behalf of the state and forced their neighbours to pay them tribute.

After he had defeated King Jie of the Xia around 1600 BCE, Cheng Tang became the first king of the Shang dynasty. The precise dates of his rule are unknown, but archaeologists believe that he founded a capital city at Bo (modern-day Shangqiu City in Henan Province). After Cheng Tang, the following eight Shang kings also ruled from the city.

Cheng Tang had learnt from the mistakes of Jie. Aided by his adviser Yi Yin, Tang ruled the Shang with kindness and compassion. Under his rule, the state flourished. Tang also expanded his empire through warfare, conquering the Di and Qiang peoples to the west. The Shang took prisoners of war and forced them to work as slaves within the state. Cheng Tang's main priority was ensuring that his subjects had enough food to eat.

The Shang's ability to make bronze objects such as this container marked them out from many neighbouring peoples.

Feeding the People

During the early Shang period, farming techniques had developed very little from the **prehistoric** Longshan era (c. 3000–2000 BCE). Peasants still used stone hoes with wooden handles to prepare the soil for planting. They harvested the grain with stone **sickles**. The most important crop was millet, but farmers also knew how to grow barley, rice and wheat. They did not have any **irrigation** techniques, however, so they did not grow rice in **paddy fields**, like later Chinese farmers.

During the Longshan era, Chinese farmers had worked for themselves. Under the Shang, life was different. All land belonged to the Shang king, and workers were organised into large labour gangs that served on the many royal farms. All grain went to the king, who redistributed it to the people. Grain was so important that conquered people had to send the Shang grain as a form of tribute.

Archaeologists uncover Shang artifacts at a site at Jinsha, near Chengdu in the south-western province of Sichuan.

Dating the Shang

In 1996 the government of the People's Republic of China set up a special project to try to establish the time frame of the Shang and Xia dynasties, together with the Zhou dynasty that followed the Shang. Some 200 scholars worked on the project for four years. They decided that the Xia had emerged around 2070 BCE and the Shang in about 1600 BCE. They were only able to establish precise dates for the last nine Shang rulers, from 1250 to 1046 BCE, when they were replaced by the Zhou.

This bronze axe was made as a weapon rather than a tool. Bronze was valuable, so most farm tools were made from stone or wood.

Using Bronze

For some historians, it was the discovery of bronze – made by mixing tin and copper – that transformed China from a Neolithic ('Stone Age') culture into a sophisticated civilisation. Bronze could be used to make weapons, tools and containers, and the Shang were the first people to **cast** bronze on a large scale. Bronze was prized because it was hard-wearing, and the Shang also became skilled in decorating bronze items.

A Royal City

Nothing remains of the first Shang capital of Bo, but historians think it probably resembled the later Shang capital at Yin (present-day Anyang City, Henan Province). In the case of Yin, the city's buildings were largely constructed from pounded earth. A defensive earth wall probably surrounded the royal palaces and religious buildings.

Only the king and members of the extended royal family lived in the city. Everyone else lived in villages outside Bo. They lived in small dwellings dug into the earth, with **wattle and daub** walls and a thatched roof. The different classes of society were also divided in death. Among the most distinctive features of the Shang

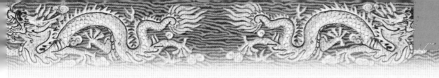
dynasty are the elaborate tombs built for the ruling **élite**. The common people living outside the city walls could be called upon at any time to excavate large areas for the tombs or build platforms and walls.

A Period of Chaos

The stability that marked the reign of Cheng Tang carried on under the kings who followed him, thanks largely to a series of wise royal advisers. But from the 10th king, Zhong Ding (ruled c. 1562–1550 BCE), the dynasty began to suffer. The next nine kings struggled to keep hold of power as infighting between members of the royal family caused instability. As a result, the capital moved at least once, although no archaeological remains of any alternative capital cities have been found. Enemies threatened to overthrow Shang rule.

This colourful carved dragon decorates the roof of a Chinese temple. Images of dragons are common throughout Chinese history.

KEY PEOPLE

The Chinese Dragon

The dragon is one of China's most important symbols. It appeared on jade **amulets** during the Shang dynasty. The dragon signifies strength and vigour and became the symbol of the Chinese emperor. The Chinese believe that dragons visit Earth only occasionally to help humans. Most of the time, they spend summer flying through the heavens and winter living deep beneath the sea. Shang craftworkers represented the coiled dragon in jade and bronze.

Fertile Land

The Xia, Shang and Zhou all settled along the Yellow River. The fertile soil allowed them to grow enough crops to feed their people. Unlike in later periods where rice was the chief crop, millet was the key staple. It was made into alcohol and was boiled to make a congee, or porridge. Ground up, millet produced flour.

Order Is Restored

The 20th Shang ruler, King Pan Geng (ruled c. 1401–1374 BCE), restored stability to Shang rule. He moved the capital to Yin (present-day Anyang) and based his policies on those of the first Shang emperor, Cheng Tang. He introduced reforms to improve the lives of common people who had been mistreated by his predecessors. He rebuilt the old capital city at Bo, although he lived at Yin, which would remain the Shang capital for 273 years. Under Pan Geng's rule the Shang grew strong again, but compared with the early period of the dynasty, they now ruled a relatively small territory.

Millet was a useful crop for farmers because it ripened very quickly and produced a high volume of grain that could be used for food.

The ruins of Yin give an impression of the size of the capital created by Pan Geng. Yin was the first permanent capital in Chinese history.

Warfare

The Shang were again just one of many states living side by side on the Chinese plains. The boundaries between states shifted constantly as **alliances** were forged or broken up.

To defend their territory, the Shang needed a large army. It could number as many as 10,000 soldiers. The soldiers all fought on foot, and armies were made up of peasants, slaves and prisoners of war. The Shang used bronze to make daggers, axes, spearheads, arrowheads and helmets. Bronze produced sharp blades and gave the Shang an advantage over their rivals who did not use bronze.

A Lack of Records

The Shang were never forgotten. Their name and the story of the fall of the dynasty were mentioned in Zhou texts. No one knew who they were, though, or what contribution they made to Chinese history. For centuries, however, there was no archaeological evidence to support the texts. Cities no longer stood, and objects made from materials such as silk and bamboo had perished over thousands of years.

The Height of the Empire

The Shang dynasty reached its height about 400 years after its founding. Its great warrior king, Wu Ding, based his policies on those of the first Shang ruler, Cheng Tang.

The greatest Shang king was the 22nd ruler of the dynasty, King Wu Ding (ruled c. 1238–1180 BCE). Wu Ding is said to have reigned for 59 years, making him the longest ruling of all the Shang kings. When he **inherited** the kingdom, it was in disarray. His uncle, King Pan Geng, had moved the capital to Yin. Wu Ding kept Yin as his capital.

A Wise Ruler

According to later Chinese accounts, King Wu Ding was a particularly wise ruler. Legend says that he did not speak for

The Yellow River gets its name from the colour of the muddy silt it carries, which it deposited in the plains where the Shang lived.

three years after he came to the throne. The reason was that before he began ruling, he first wanted to observe the kingdom and work out the best way to reign. He wanted to follow the principles of the first Shang king, Cheng Tang.

The legend continues that Wu Ding wanted a sage, or wise adviser. One night he dreamt of a sage named Yue and searched the kingdom until he found Yue, who was a slave rather than a member of the élite. With Yue's guidance, Wu Ding brought the Shang dynasty to its peak.

This model shows the kind of wooden framework Shang builders would have used to construct walls of rammed earth.

This chariot found in a tomb in Yin contains the skeletons of horses sacrificed so they could pull the chariot in the afterlife.

Coming of the Chariot

The Shang started using the wheeled chariot in around 1200 BCE. The two-wheeled vehicle was pulled by two horses and was made from wood or basketwork. The Shang imported the idea of the chariot from the Steppe peoples to the west, with whom they traded. Shang nobles used chariots for hunting, but later they were also used to carry archers into battle.

Shang Territory Expands

Wu Ding set out to expand the amount of territory under Shang control. During his long reign, the Shang came to control much of eastern China and also west, beyond the Taihang Mountains, a tall ragged range that runs north to south in north-eastern China.

The expansion of their territory brought the Shang into contact with new peoples from the west and new inventions, such as the **chariot**. Historians know more about this period in Shang history than about the earlier dynasty because of a number of significant discoveries at the old Shang capital Yin (Anyang).

The Dynastic Capital

Under Wu Ding, Yin was a magnificent ceremonial centre with royal palaces, temples and houses contained within its defensive city walls. Its buildings had solid earth floors and walls of packed earth, with wooden pillars supporting thatched roofs. Workshops to cast bronze or prepare animal bones for writing were located outside Yin's walls.

Members of the extended royal family – which was very large and had many branches – lived in Yin because they were required to carry out religious rituals there. Other nobles lived in their own towns beyond the capital: the most important nobles governed the largest towns. Yin was home to many ceremonial tombs. By 2014,

These bones belonged to some of the 16 human sacrifices buried at Yin with the Shang queen Lady Fu Hao. Her tomb was discovered in 1976.

A New Capital

The Shang had as many as eight capital cities, but most have disappeared without trace. The first Shang king, Chang Teng, made Bo his capital. The 10th king Zhong Ding moved it to Ao, near present-day Zhengzhou in Henan Province. In 1384 BCE, Pan Geng moved the capital to Yin. Yin remained the Shang capital until it was destroyed when King Di Xin was overthrown in 1046 BCE.

This bronze bell carries the face of a hideous Taotie. Many bronze items were decorated in a similar way, but we do not understand why.

archaeologists digging at Anyang had unearthed at least 13 royal tombs, together with more than 2,000 smaller tombs and pits for **sacrifices**. The most famous royal tomb belonged to Lady Fu Hao. She was said to have been one of the wives of Wu Ding. It is the only Shang royal tomb to have been discovered intact and was uncovered in 1976.

Expansion through Warfare

The contents of Lady Fu Hao's tomb confirm the evidence of thousands of oracle bones and **inscriptions** on bronze vessels about the importance of warfare. During the reign of Wu Ding, war was the chief means for the Shang to increase territory, gain prisoners to work for the empire and increase the amount of tribute they received from conquered peoples. The conquered peoples usually paid tribute in the form of grain, such as millet, or cattle, but they also sent people to the Shang as slaves. The Shang particularly prized copper and tin, which were needed for bronze casting, and turtle shells that were used for divination purposes.

BELIEFS

The Taotie

The Taotie was a common motif on Shang bronze vessels and later on Zhou vessels. The Taotie was half-human and half-animal and was ugly. It had wide eyes that bulged and a long nose. Some Taotie had fangs, horns, legs and tails. They usually appeared on ceremonial vessels, but archaeologists do not know what they represented.

Military Power

The Shang army, which was led by the king, had become a formidable force. Soldiers were divided into companies of 100 men, and were usually infantry or archers. Archers used bows made from wood, bone and horn. The bows became the standard weapon of the **nomadic** peoples who lived on the **steppes** of Central Asia. Known in Europe as the Turkish bow, the Shang bow was more powerful than Western bows. It could kill at a range of 183 metres (200 yards). Despite such a range, however, most

Mandate in Heaven

The Zhou dynasty that overthrew the Shang in 1046 BCE sought to legitimise their action with a concept named the Mandate of Heaven. The concept argued that only the virtuous could rule, and that if a dynasty was corrupt in any way, it could be overthrown. This became the guiding principle by which China was governed for centuries: when a dynasty failed its people, it was replaced by a new dynasty. All founding emperors were seen as strong and all last emperors as weak and corrupt.

A stone in Anyang marks the place where the world's largest ancient bronze was found. It was a square ding, or vessel, 133 centimetres (4 feet 4 inches) tall with four legs.

The home of simuwu ding

fighting was still carried out hand-to-hand by foot soldiers. The ruling élite fought alongside the ordinary soldiers.

Lady Fu Hao and Her Tomb

Shang kings had many wives and many children. Lady Fu Hao was one of Wu Ding's three main queens. When her tomb was discovered in 1976, archaeologists found other skeletons inside it. Historians believe they belonged to human sacrifices who may have been killed to accompany the queen in the **afterlife**. The tomb also included valuable objects made from bronze and jade. In addition, the tomb held 4,000 cowrie shells. The Shang used cowrie shells as money, so this suggested Fu Hao was wealthy.

The Shang sometimes buried chariots and horses with their royal owners. Lady Fu Hao's tomb contained a number of chariots, reflecting one of the most remarkable facts that historians know about her. Lady Fu Hao was an experienced military commander. She went into battle at the head of an army of 13,000 men, which was far larger than normal Shang armies. Lady Fu Hao was also involved in negotiating peace

This statue of Lady Fu Hao shows her ready to lead her army to war, but the statue is quite modern so it may be an idealised portrait.

DAILY LIFE

The Calendar

Shang ritual was based on an accurate calendar. Astronomers observed the Moon to divide the lunar year into 12 months of 29 or 30 days. To remain linked to the solar calendar of 365 days, an extra week was added every seven years. An accurate calendar was vital for successful harvests. It told people when to plant and harvest their crops.

Royal Tombs

Tombs were a way for Shang rulers to demonstrate their power and wealth. Kings filled their tombs with useful items, luxuries and money. These were to be used by the dead person and show that the Shang believed in some form of afterlife. The fact that Yin (Anyang) has so many royal tombs (13) has led historians to believe that it was the most important of the Shang capital cities.

treaties with other tribes and she conducted important religious ceremonies, some of which involved animal and human sacrifice.

Rituals

The Shang believed that the king's principal role was to carry out all kinds of religious rituals. There were different forms of ritual. Some paid respect to Shang ancestors, others kept the gods happy and others foretold the future using oracle bones. This was how the king and his advisers looked for confirmation from the gods that they were following the correct course of action. King Wu Ding was celebrated for the number of his rituals. This contrasted with the last Shang king, Di Xin (ruled 1075–1046 BCE), who was disliked by the people because he did not carry out enough rituals.

The tomb of Lady Fu Hao contained 468 bronze objects, 755 jade objects and many pieces of pottery, bone, stone, ivory and shell.

The Peoples of the Empire

Just as we know little about the Shang, we know little about their neighbouring peoples, but all these peoples seem to have had quite highly structured societies.

The Shang were just one of many tribes that settled close to the Yellow River in the early Bronze Age. Because only later accounts survive of most aspects of everyday Shang life, however, it is difficult for modern historians to work out the different relationships between the Shang and their immediate neighbours.

Shang Society

More is known about the structure of Shang society. It was dominated by the idea of rank and status. Society was structured like a pyramid, with the king alone at the top. The other layers from the top down included members of the royal family, then the nobles, advisers and

These Shang pottery figures depict prisoners of war, who were likely to end up as slaves or human sacrifices.

順天應人　本乎仁義
以質維忠　匪曰求異
盤銘一德　杀林六事
人紀肇修　垂千萬岳
湯

KEY PEOPLE

Slaves

Slaves were vital to the Shang state. Some 5 per cent of the population were slaves. They were usually prisoners of war. They had no rights and could not be freed. Slaves did many jobs. They were used on farms to prepare the fields for planting. They also dug the royal tombs – some were sacrificed and buried alongside their noble owners.

priests. The next layer included craftworkers, merchants and farmers, with slaves at the bottom. Slaves were often not Shang but came instead from neighbouring tribes. The Shang and their neighbours were **ethnically** similar, however – in some cases, tribes were related to the Shang through marriage – so slaves may not have looked different from their masters.

Male Shang nobles held specialised jobs in the government and the army. These were passed down through generations of a

This image shows Cheng Tang, who had originally established the importance of the ruler within Shang society.

Shaping beautiful jade objects took many hours of laborious work, so jade carvers were highly prized.

family. This early division of society according to social rank carried on from the Shang into much later Chinese dynasties, such as the Han and the Ming.

Other Tribes

The Shang gave their rival tribes the collective name of 'Fang'. The Shang's relationship with the different tribes of Fang changed over time: at some periods they were friendly, but at other times they were at war. We only know about the different Fang groups from mentions of their names on oracle bones. We do know, however, that the Shang lived under permanent threat of attack, either from the Fang or from nomadic tribes from the Asian steppes. The Shang kept a permanent army on standby to defend themselves.

The different Fang tribes included the Kung Fang, who lived in north-west China. They were not a major threat to

KEY PEOPLE

Artisans

Although craftworkers occupied a low place in Shang society, they were valued because of their skills at working bronze and jade. The skills were passed on from father to son. As well as making everyday objects, workers spent months creating objects to be placed in royal tombs. Craftworkers lived in their own cities outside the royal city.

the Shang, however, because when the Shang attacked them they did so with an army of only 6,000 men. Another group, the Ch'iang Fang, lived somewhere west of the Shang but the exact location is not known. They are the only people mentioned in Shang writings as being suppliers of sacrificial victims for rituals connected with **ancestor worship**. The Shang often invaded the Ch'iang Fang with armies of up to 13,000 men. (This may have been the army led by Lady Fu Hao.) Fighting another tribe, the Jen Fang, ultimately weakened the Shang and allowed the Zhou to conquer them.

KEY PEOPLE

Peasants

Peasants were at the bottom of Shang society but they were essential. They grew the crops – such as millet, wheat, rice and corn – that were crucial to the survival of the dynasty. Although the Shang were skilled bronze workers, most peasants had only stone or wooden tools. They lived in modest settlements outside the royal city.

The kind of small villages where Shang peasants lived may have resembled similar rural Chinese villages today.

Life in the Empire

The state controlled many aspects of Shang life. Shang nobles lived a life of luxury that created work for the craftworkers and weavers who made striking objects for them.

Since the discovery of Lady Fu Hao's tomb in 1976, ongoing archaeological excavations there and elsewhere have revealed more information about life in the Late Shang period. It is better understood than any other period of the Shang dynasty.

An Agricultural Society

Although the Shang were one of the first societies in the world to live in urban centres, their economy was built on farming. Despite lacking any irrigation techniques or metal tools, Shang farmers were able to produce a surplus of grain to support the urban population.

Among the items found in Lady Fu Hao's tomb was a pot probably used to cook rice and dates. Unlike in later Chinese cultures, rice was not

Priests called diviners wrote messages on oracle bones, which were usually made from the shoulders of cattle or from turtle shells.

a staple food for the Shang. Most ordinary Shang ate millet and wheat, along with vegetables and fruit. Fish and meat were limited mainly to the wealthy who could afford them. The same cooking techniques used by the Shang – stir-frying, deep-frying and steaming – are still the most common ways of cooking in China. The Shang ate with chopsticks, as the Chinese still do today.

The Shang were familiar with animals that have long since become extinct in China, such as elephants, rhinoceroses and tigers. The king and his male nobles hunted and ate them. The Shang held banquets with

Shang bronze vessels were used in religious rituals, but were also used in everyday life by the wealthier members of society.

Silk is produced by boiling cocoons produced by the larvae of the silk moth and unravelling the fine threads.

Production of Silk

Silk was made in China before the Shang, but historians believe the Shang perfected its production. Silk was so expensive it was used only for the royal family and nobles. It took 2,000 silkworms to produce around 500 grams (1 pound) of silk. The Shang made a form of paper from silk and used it to write on, but no Shang silk survives today.

large amounts of food and wine to honour their ancestors. Wine cups found in tombs suggest that wine may also have been used for religious ceremonies.

Rituals and Ancestors

The king was at the heart of the state religion, and he performed the many rituals the Shang believed were necessary to please the gods and maintain harmony in society. The Shang worshipped Shang Di as the supreme god and believed that only a king could communicate with him. They also worshipped minor nature gods who ruled the Sun, Moon, wind and rain.

Tombs and Funeral Rites

The Shang also practised ancestor worship and believed in life after death. When a person died, the Shang believed he or she continued to influence and help living family members. To keep the ancestors

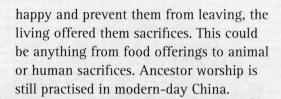

happy and prevent them from leaving, the living offered them sacrifices. This could be anything from food offerings to animal or human sacrifices. Ancestor worship is still practised in modern-day China.

When a Shang noble died, he or she was buried with everything for the afterlife. This included not only vessels for food and drink but also servants to prepare and serve food, because the Shang believed a cook would still be a cook in the afterlife.

The most elaborate tombs belonged to members of the royal family. Lady Fu Hao's tomb contained more than 400

DAILY LIFE

Shell Money

The Shang used the shells of cowries, or sea snails, as a form of money. Eventually the natural supply of cowrie shells from the coast ran out, so people started to make imitation shells from bone, horn, bronze or other materials. The distribution of cowrie shells in China has helped archaeologists to study the rise and fall of the Shang.

Silk can be dyed to create bright colours. It can then be woven into intricate patterns. However, no silk has survived from the Shang period.

This pit of oracle bones was found during excavations at Yin. The number of bones suggests how widespread the practice of divination was.

Music

Shang musicians took part in religious ceremonies, but music was also used to entertain the royal family and its officials. The Shang had one of the earliest forms of orchestra, although no written music has survived. The musicians played bronze *nao* bells in sets of three or five bells of differing sizes, pan pipes made from hollow tubes and bone pipes. They also played cymbals and drums made from bronze.

bronze objects. A Shang king might be buried with bronze and jade objects, silk, chariots, cowrie shells and oracle bones.

To construct impressive royal tombs, thousands of labourers – often slaves – were put to work to dig holes as deep as 12 metres (40 feet) into the ground. Then they used wood to divide the tomb into burial chambers: the wealthier the dead person, the more burial chambers in the tomb.

A Wealthy People

Historians believe the Shang dynasty was well off compared with its neighbours because of the large number of bronze objects found at Shang sites. Bronze was expensive to make and cast, and the highly decorated Shang bronzes were luxury possessions. The Shang traded bronzes with other tribes for food or raw materials. They were also highly valued gifts among the Shang.

Jade is a hard, green stone that has traditionally been valued for its beautiful colour, its **durability** and its smooth finish. The Shang prized it as a symbol of immortal life. Because jade is very hard and the Shang did not have tools that could cut it, they ground the stone using sand mixed with water. The process was very time-consuming and highly skilled, which made jade objects expensive to create. Shang craftworkers shaped jade into exquisite objects. Lady Hao's tomb, for example, included tiny jade dragons.

Oracle bones carry two sets of markings: the cracks produced by heating the bones, and the priests' record of what the cracks mean.

Discovering the Oracle Bones

In 1899, farmers from Anyang tried to sell Wang Yirong, an antiques dealer, 'dragon bones', an ingredient in traditional medicine. Before the bones could be ground into medicine, Wang Yirong realised they were the shoulder blades of cattle and turtle shells – and they were covered in writing. The find drew archaeologists to Anyang, where thousands of bones revealed the location of the ancient Shang capital.

Chinese Writing

The writing system created by the Shang developed gradually over centuries into the system used in modern China. During the Qin dynasty (221–206 BCE), the characters used by the Shang were fixed as the basis of the writtten language. In 1716, the *Kangxi Dictionary* was published with 47,000 characters. To be considered fully literate, a Chinese person today needs to know between 3,000 and 4,000 characters.

Writing

Along with their technological advances in metalworking and warfare, the Shang also invented Chinese writing. They created a set of characters, which represent sounds, and pictograms, which represent ideas. These symbols are still used as the basis of Chinese writing today and have changed remarkably little since the Shang invented them. The Shang wrote on strips of bamboo or on silk, but such materials have rotted away a long time ago. Historians believe they used writing not only to keep official records but also to record their poetry. During the reign of King Wu Ding, as bronze work became more sophisticated, the sides of bronze objects often bore engraved inscriptions.

The Shang began the practice of writing on strips of bamboo; it continues today, as illustrated here.

Joss sticks burn in front of an altar dedicated to ancestor worship, which was a practice started by the Shang.

Oracle Bones

The objects that have given historians most information about the Shang are oracle bones. The Shang wrote questions about the future on turtle shells or cattle bones. The shells and bones were then used in a ritual that was either performed in the presence of the king by a priest known as a **diviner** or was carried out by the king himself. The priest or king scraped dips in the reverse side of the bone or shell, and sometimes dripped blood on it. Then he heated a rod that he pushed into the hollows he had made. The heat caused the bone or shell to crack. The diviner then interpreted the cracks to learn the gods' answer, and wrote the answer on the shell or bone as a record.

BELIEFS

I Ching and Maths

The *I Ching* is an ancient Chinese handbook for divination, or telling the future, using random numbers in groups of six called hexagrams. Although the work dates from the time of the Zhou, who overthrew the Shang, historians think it contains Shang ideas. Shang diviners and mathematicians used the 64 hexagrams set out in the book. The Shang were also some of the first people to use the decimal system for maths.

Fall of the Empire

The Chinese believed that all dynasties begin well and end badly, when they are overthrown by a new dynasty. This pattern was evident in the downfall of the Shang.

Historians have identified at least 26 states that neighboured Shang territory at one time or another. During the golden age of King Wu Ding, the Shang had fought these peoples, or Fang, in order to expand their territory and increase the amount of tribute they received. Around 1100 BCE, however, the Gongfang fought back, defeating the later Shang kings. The Gongfang reclaimed territory until the region under Shang control shrank to the relatively small area immediately around the capital at Yin (Anyang). Once again, the Shang were

This stone carving of a Taoist ritual was created in about 572 BCE under the Zhou, who overthrew the Shang in 1046 BCE.

These terraced fields in Hunan Province were dug for growing rice, which became the staple crop of southern China by 750 CE.

just one of a number of competing states. Boundaries and alliances shifted constantly and wars were common.

The Last Shang King

According to historical accounts, King Di Xin (ruled c. 1075–1046 BCE) began his rule well. Wanting to reinforce Shang power in the Yangtze Valley, Di Xin led two major expeditions against the troublesome Renfang. He also led another campaign against the Yufang, former allies of the Shang whose territory lay north-east of Yin. The fact that the king was able to mobilise large numbers of men to fight in three major military

This painting shows the 10th-century BCE Zhou king Wu Mang being entertained by a musician.

campaigns suggests that the Shang state was still a force to be reckoned with.

To the west, King Wen of the Zhou dynasty (ruled c. 1099–1050 BCE) was a vassal of the Shang and paid tribute to them. Di Xin gave him the title 'Count of the West' and ordered Wen to help in his battles. As Di Xin's reign continued, however, he became concerned about King Wen's increasing popularity and imprisoned him.

Wen was later released, but tensions grew between the Shang and the Zhou. Meanwhile, Di Xin grew corrupt and cruel and he became unpopular among the Shang. Wen began to build a power base by making allies among enemies of the Shang, but he died in 1050 BCE before he could challenge Din Xi directly.

The Longest Dynasty

The Zhou were one of the many neighbours of the Shang. The Zhou dynasty begun by King Wu when he defeated the Shang lasted longer than any other dynasty in Chinese history, from 1046 to 256 BCE. Strong central power lasted under the so-called Western Zhou until 771 BCE. Under the Eastern Zhou who followed, the power of the state declined. By 481 BCE, Zhou territory had split into many independent states.

King Wen was succeeded by his son, Wu (ruled 1049–1043 BCE). The new king waited before launching a revolt against the Shang. According to the concept of the Mandate of Heaven, if Wu attacked at just the right moment to overthrow a corrupt ruler, the attack would be justified.

The Battle of Muye

On 26 January 1046 BCE, King Wu of Zhou led an army of around 50,000 men towards Yin. The Shang army was fighting a war in the east, but Di Xin still had 530,000 men available to defend his capital. In order to make sure of victory, King Di Xin had armed 170,000 slaves to

The Legacy of the Shang

The first Chinese dynasty left a remarkable legacy. The Shang introduced a writing system, bronze, accurate lunar and solar calendars and ancestor worship. All of these have become central to Chinese culture, but it is only in the last century that they have been identified as the legacy of the Shang thanks to major archaeological discoveries and ongoing research.

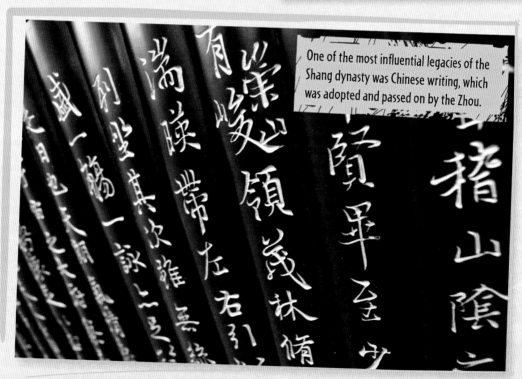

One of the most influential legacies of the Shang dynasty was Chinese writing, which was adopted and passed on by the Zhou.

Ongoing Discoveries

The discovery of the oracle bones in 1899 and Lady Fu Hao's tomb in 1976 are two of the most spectacular archaeological finds in history. Much of our knowledge about the Shang, however, comes from more everyday work at different Shang sites. One of the most important is Yin, where the royal tombs still yield new artifacts. In 1999, archaeologists uncovered a pool at the royal palace where Di Xin killed himself.

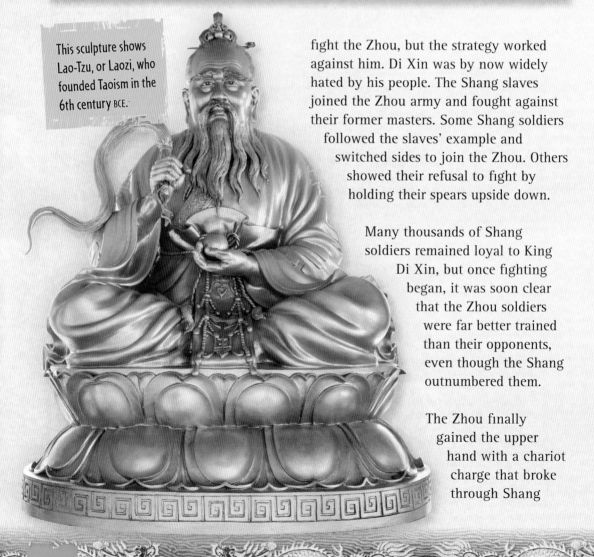

This sculpture shows Lao-Tzu, or Laozi, who founded Taoism in the 6th century BCE.

fight the Zhou, but the strategy worked against him. Di Xin was by now widely hated by his people. The Shang slaves joined the Zhou army and fought against their former masters. Some Shang soldiers followed the slaves' example and switched sides to join the Zhou. Others showed their refusal to fight by holding their spears upside down.

Many thousands of Shang soldiers remained loyal to King Di Xin, but once fighting began, it was soon clear that the Zhou soldiers were far better trained than their opponents, even though the Shang outnumbered them.

The Zhou finally gained the upper hand with a chariot charge that broke through Shang lines. King Di Xin fled, leaving his soldiers without a commander. In the chaos that followed, the Zhou soldiers easily defeated the demoralised Shang.

The only accounts that survive of the battle are from Zhou sources, so they may be biased (favour one side). They report that King Di Xin returned to his palace, where he covered himself in jewels before lighting a fire in the Deer Terrace Pavilion and burning himself to death.

After the battle, the victorious King Wu made sure the Shang dynasty could not return by executing Di Xin's wife, Daji. But Wu released Shang officials without punishing them, and some of the royal advisers even went to work for the Zhou dynasty. The people were starving, which was one reason they had turned on Di Xin, so King Wu ordered the opening of the imperial rice store to feed them. The Shang dynasty had ended. The Zhou were now in control.

BELIEFS

Chinese Religions

Shang values influenced later Chinese beliefs. Confucianism took the form of rules of behaviour devised by the scholar Confucius (c. 551–479 BCE). The rules were based on ancestor worship; people owed loyalty to their family and their elders. Taoism, which developed between 600 and 500 BCE, stressed the importance of balance. That reflected the concept of the Mandate of Heaven, which balanced good and poor rule.

Confucian beliefs still underpin Chinese life. The Imperial Vault of Heaven is a Confucian temple built in Beijing in 1530.

Timeline

c. 3000 BCE The beginning of the Longshan era marks the emergence of Neolithic cultures in China.

c. 2070 BCE The Xia emerge as the leading people in the plains of north-central China.

c. 1700 BCE The settlement at Erlitou is occupied by the late Xia or the early Shang dynasty.

c. 1600 BCE The Shang defeat the Xia in the Battle of Mingtiao and take control of the Yellow River region. Cheng Tang becomes the first king of the Shang dynasty.

1562 BCE The 10th Shang emperor, Zhong Ding, comes to the throne; he rules until 1550 BCE. He moves the capital from Bo to Ao, in present-day Henan Province.

c. 1401 BCE King Pan Geng comes to the throne around this time. He restores stability to the Shang after a period of turmoil and moves the Shang capital from Ao to Yin (Anyang).

c. 1250 The earliest-known written Chinese records, written on oracle bones, date from around this time.

c. 1238 BCE   Around this time, Wu Ding becomes the 22nd Shang king, and one of the greatest. His 59-year reign is the longest of any Shang ruler.

c. 1200 BCE   The chariot is introduced to the Shang by nomadic peoples to the west.

c. 1200 BCE   Lady Fu Hao, a queen of Wu Ding, is buried in a tomb full of personal possessions. Oracle bones provide the first evidence of the Chinese calendar.

c. 1122 BCE   The Zhou dynasty is founded on the edge of the Shang empire.

c. 1075 BCE   Xi Din becomes the last Shang ruler.

1050 BCE   King Wen of Zhou dies before he can launch an attack on the Shang.

1049 BCE   Wu succeeds his father as king of the Zhou.

1046 BCE   The Zhou overthrow the last Shang king, Di Xin, in the Battle of Muye.

Glossary

afterlife A form of life that some people believe continues after death.

alliances Agreements between states to cooperate to achieve certain goals.

amulets Small pieces of jewellery believed to offer the wearer protection against bad luck.

ancestor worship Rituals to ask dead ancestors to help the living.

bronze A yellow–brown metal made by mixing molten copper with tin.

cast To shape metal by melting it and pouring it into a mould.

chariot A two-wheeled vehicle pulled by horses.

chronicles Written accounts of historical events.

diviner Someone who uses various ways to foretell the future.

durability The ability to resist wear.

dynasty A series of rulers who are members of the same family.

élite A group of important or influential people.

ethnically Relating to a people's common racial or cultural qualities.

exile Being banished from one's own country, usually as a punishment.

inherited Something received from someone who has died.

inscriptions Marks or words scratched into a hard surface.

irrigation Diverting water in order to helps crops grow.

Neolithic Relating to the late part of the Stone Age.

nomadic Having no fixed home.

oracle bones Small pieces of animal bone or turtle shell used by the Shang to foretell the future.

paddy fields Flooded fields where rice is grown.

prehistoric Belonging to the time before written records.

sacrifices Offerings made to the gods.

sickles Tools with curved blades for cutting crops.

steppes Large, flat areas of grassland.

tribute Payment made by one ruler to another.

vassal A country or person that is subordinate to another.

wattle and daub A building material made by weaving sticks together and then covering them with mud.

Further Reading

Books

Barker, Geoffrey, *The Shang Dynasty of Ancient China* (The History Detective Investigates), Wayland, 2014.

Brooks, Susie, *China* (Unpacked), Wayland, 2015.

Kelly, Tracey, *Shang Dynasty China* (Great Civilisations), Franklin Watts, 2014.

Samuels, Charlie, *The Shang and other Chinese Dynasties* (Technology in the Ancient World), Franklin Watts, 2015.

Steele, Philip, *Empires* (Epic!), Wayland, 2015.

Websites

Ancient China – The British Museum
www.ancientchina.co.uk/menu.html
Pages about ancient China from the British Museum, with games and activities.

Ducksters.com
www.ducksters.com/history/china/shang_dynasty.php
Ducksters page about the Shang dynasty with links to many aspects of ancient China.

Mr Donn
china.mrdonn.org/shang&chou.html
Introduction to the Shang and Zhou dynasties from Mr Donn's learning site.

Index